SHARKS and CLEANER FISH

By Janey Levy

Gareth Stevens
PUBLISHING

Please visit our website, www.garethstevens.com. For a free color catalog of all our high-quality books, call toll free 1-800-542-2595 or fax 1-877-542-2596.

Library of Congress Cataloging-in-Publication Data

Names: Levy, Janey, author.
Title: Sharks and cleaner fish / Janey Levy.
Description: New York : Gareth Stevens Publishing, [2022] | Series: Animal pals | Includes index.
Identifiers: LCCN 2020036693 (print) | LCCN 2020036694 (ebook) | ISBN 9781538266939 (library binding) | ISBN 9781538266915 (paperback) | ISBN 9781538266922 (set) | ISBN 9781538266946 (ebook)
Subjects: LCSH: Sharks–Juvenile literature. | Cleaner fishes–Juvenile literature. | Mutualism (Biology)–Juvenile literature.
Classification: LCC QL638.9 .L515 2022 (print) | LCC QL638.9 (ebook) | DDC 597.3/3–dc23
LC record available at https://lccn.loc.gov/2020036693
LC ebook record available at https://lccn.loc.gov/2020036694

First Edition

Published in 2022 by
Gareth Stevens Publishing
29 E. 21st Street
New York, NY 10010

Copyright © 2022 Gareth Stevens Publishing

Designer: Andrea Davison-Bartolotta
Editor: Monika Davies

Photo credits: Cover (top), p. 1 (top) Alastair Pollock/500Px Plus/Getty Images; cover (bottom), p. 1 (bottom) shrub/iStock/Getty Images; p. 5 Alastair Pollock Photography/Moment/Getty Images; p. 7 (main) Brent Durand/Moment/Getty Images; p. 7 (top left inset) Gerard Soury/Stockbyte/Getty Images; p. 7 (top right inset) 3dsam79/iStock/Getty Images Plus/Getty Images; p. 7 (bottom inset) Dmitry Miroshnikov/Moment/Getty Images; p. 9 Norbert Probst/Getty Images; p. 10 scubadesign/Shutterstock.com; p. 11 Michael Weberberger/Getty Images; p. 12 Andrea Izzotti/Shutterstock.com; p. 13 (main) Cat Gennaro/Moment/Getty Images; p. 13 (inset) Rodrigo Friscione/Image Source/Getty Images; p. 15 Jakob Ziegler/iStock/Getty Images Plus/Getty Images; p. 17 (map) Andrei Minsk/Shutterstock.com; p. 17 (inset) marrio31/iStock/Getty Images Plus/Getty Images; p. 19 Reinhard Dirscherl/ullstein bild/Getty Images; p. 20 Imagine Earth Photorapy/Shutterstock.com; p. 21 Andrey Nekrasov/Getty Images.

Printed in the United States of America

CPSIA compliance information: Batch #CSGS22: For further information contact Gareth Stevens, New York, New York at 1-800-542-2595.

Find us on

FISH FRIENDS

Sharks have a scary **reputation**. The word "shark" often strikes terror in people's hearts. Many ocean creatures also avoid this well-known predator. But did you know there are some fish that actually hang out with sharks?

Several species, or kinds, of cleaner fish spend a lot of time near sharks. Cleaner fish get benefits from their close **relationship** with sharks, and sharks don't eat them. Sharks usually benefit from the relationship too. You'll learn lots more about different kinds of sharks and cleaner fish inside this book.

FACT FINDER!

A mutualistic relationship is a relationship between two different kinds of animals that benefits both of them.

CONTENTS

Words in the glossary appear in **bold** type the first time they are used in the text.

Sharks are not as scary as their reputation suggests. When they bite people, it is often because they are curious. They don't usually eat people.

SAY HI TO SHARKS

When you think of sharks, you might picture huge fish with a mouth filled with sharp teeth. But there are around 500 species of sharks, and not all of them are scary. Some sharks are as small as a human hand. And the largest shark—the whale shark—only eats tiny animals and plants floating in the ocean!

However, all sharks share certain common features. Their **skeleton** is made of bendable matter called cartilage, not bones. Toothlike scales cover their skin. Many sharks must swim continually to avoid sinking.

FACT FINDER!

Sharks are found in all sorts of ocean **habitats**. They live around **coral reefs** in warm waters, deep down in the ocean, and in cold Arctic waters!

Sharks come in different shapes, sizes, and even colors. The goblin shark can be bright pink!

reef shark

dogfish shark

goblin shark

hammerhead shark

SWIMMING WITH SHARKS

Warm ocean waters are home to oceanic whitetip sharks. These scary predators' meals include bony fish, sea turtles—and even other sharks! Yet you'll often see several small striped fish swimming along beside them. Are these little fish brave or foolish?

The sharks won't eat these small fish, called pilot fish. Why not? It's because pilot fish are cleaner fish. They eat **parasites** off the sharks' skin. Small pilot fish may even swim into a shark's mouth to clean out bits of food. That's wild!

Oceanic whitetip sharks can grow to be 13 feet (4 m) long. Pilot fish are often only about 1 foot (0.3 m) long.

FACT FINDER!

A cleaner fish is a smaller fish that cleans parasites off a larger fish. There are many kinds of cleaner fish in the sea.

IS IT MUTUALISM?

By swimming alongside big, scary sharks, pilot fish are **protected** from other ocean predators that might want to eat them. The sharks benefit, too, from the cleaning the pilot fish provide. But do they have a mutualistic relationship?

Some scientists say the relationship is commensalism. That's a relationship where one creature benefits and the other gets little in the way of either benefit or harm. These scientists think pilot fish benefit greatly from the relationship while sharks benefit only a little. What do you think?

FACT FINDER!

Pilot fish swim with sea turtles and other kinds of sharks as well.

Oceanic whitetip sharks are in danger of **extinction**.
What will happen to pilot fish if the sharks disappear?

HITCHING A RIDE

You might spy different kinds of sharks swimming around with small fish stuck to them. How weird is that?

These small fish are another kind of cleaner fish. They are called remoras. A remora sticks itself to a shark using a special disk on its head! This helps the remora get a ride on the shark, as well as protection from predators. The remora also eats food scraps from the shark's meals and may sometimes clean parasites off the shark.

remora

remora's suction disk

Remoras are usually from 1 to 3 feet (0.3 to 0.9 m) long.

WHAT KIND OF RELATIONSHIP?

Remoras benefit greatly from their relationship with sharks. What do sharks get out of it?

Sometimes, remoras eat parasites off sharks. It may seem like remoras and sharks have a mutualistic relationship. But scientists think that may not be the case. Some believe the remoras are probably eating parasites that have already fallen off the shark. Remoras also likely slow down the sharks they're stuck to, causing the sharks to need more **energy** to swim.

FACT FINDER!

It's hard to say what kind of relationship remoras have with sharks. Most believe the relationship is commensalism.

The name "remora" means "something that slows down something else."

SHARK SPAS

Pilot fish and remoras seek out sharks. But sharks seek out a third type of cleaner fish: cleaner wrasses.

Cleaner wrasses are like business operators! They hang out around coral reefs, where they run "cleaning stations." Sharks visit these cleaning stations. They swim slowly, spread out their **gills**, and open their mouth to let the wrasses know they want to be cleaned. The wrasses then go to work. They eat parasites, dead skin, and bits of food stuck between the shark's teeth.

FACT FINDER!

Cleaner wrasses work hard. Each one can check out over 2,000 visitors to its cleaning station each day!

Where to Find Cleaner Wrasses

bluestreak cleaner wrasse

Pacific Ocean

Indian Ocean

cleaner wrasse habitat

The common cleaner wrasse, which is also called the bluestreak cleaner wrasse, makes its home around coral reefs in the Indian and Pacific Oceans.

TRUE MUTUALISM

Sharks and cleaner wrasses have a truly mutualistic relationship. Getting rid of parasites, dead skin, and rotting food between their teeth helps improve the health of sharks. In exchange, cleaner wrasses get a tasty meal. But even here there's a catch.

If they had a choice, wrasses would eat the protective **mucus** covering the shark's skin instead of parasites. That wouldn't be helpful for the shark. So, what keeps wrasses from eating the shark's mucus? The shark chases them if they try!

FACT FINDER!

Scientists have discovered cleaner wrasses help make sharks and other fish smarter by keeping them free of parasites!

Cleaner wrasses are less likely to cheat and eat a shark's mucus if they know other sharks are watching. They don't want to scare away business!

FALSE CLEANER FISH

The world of cleaner fish—like the rest of nature—is full of surprises. It turns out there are some fish that look like cleaner fish but are not actually cleaner fish. One such fish is the false cleaner fish.

False cleaner fish look like cleaner wrasses and, like cleaner wrasses, hang out around coral reefs. Since they look like cleaner wrasses, they can easily approach sharks and other fish wanting to be cleaned. But instead of cleaning, they bite off bits of fins, scales, and skin!

coral reef

There may be false cleaner fish in the sea, but "real" cleaner fish have a real **impact** on other sea creatures. Their mutualistic relationship with sharks helps them both.

GLOSSARY

coral reef: an underwater hill made up of the hard parts of tiny sea animals

energy: the strength or power that allows you to do things

extinction: the death of all members of a species

gill: the body part that ocean animals such as fish use to breathe in water

habitat: the natural place where an animal or plant lives

impact: a strong effect

mucus: a thick slime produced by the bodies of many animals

parasite: a living thing that lives in, on, or with another living thing and often harms it

protect: to keep safe

relationship: a connection between two living things

reputation: the views that are held about something or someone

skeleton: the strong frame that supports an animal's body

FOR MORE INFORMATION

Books

Foote, Kristen. *How to Survive as a Shark*. Seattle, WA: The Innovation Press, 2017.

Schuetz, Kari. *Oceanic Whitetip Sharks and Pilot Fish*. Minneapolis, MN: Bellwether Media, 2019.

Skerry, Brian. T*he Ultimate Book of Sharks: Your Guide to These Fierce and Fantastic Fish*. Washington, DC: National Geographic Society, 2018.

Websites

Fearless Fish Cleans Shark's Mouth | Seven Worlds, One Planet | BBC Earth
www.youtube.com/watch?v=V5EszU8yuA8
Watch a great video that shows cleaner wrasses cleaning a shark's mouth.

Sharks
www.montereybayaquarium.org/animals/animals-a-to-z/sharks
Learn more about sharks and why they're important on this website.

Symbiosis
kids.britannica.com/kids/article/symbiosis/400286
Learn more about mutualistic and parasitic relationships between creatures here.

INDEX